ANIMALS AND PLANT L

CW00558413

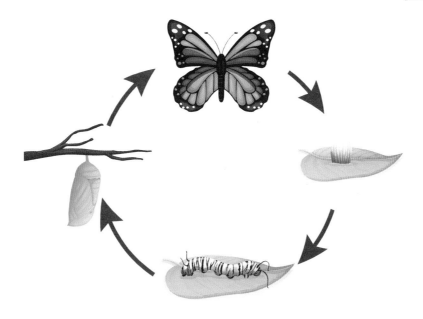

INDEX

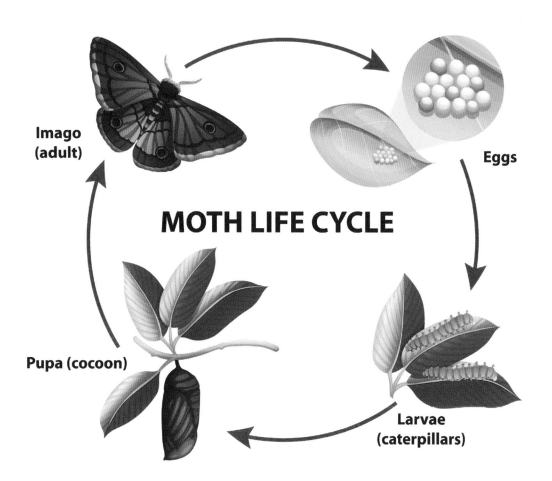

MOTH LIFE CYCLE

Imago (adult)

Eggs

Larvae (caterpillars)

Pupa (cocoon)

SILKWORM LIFE CYCLE

Larva

Pupa

Adult

Eggs

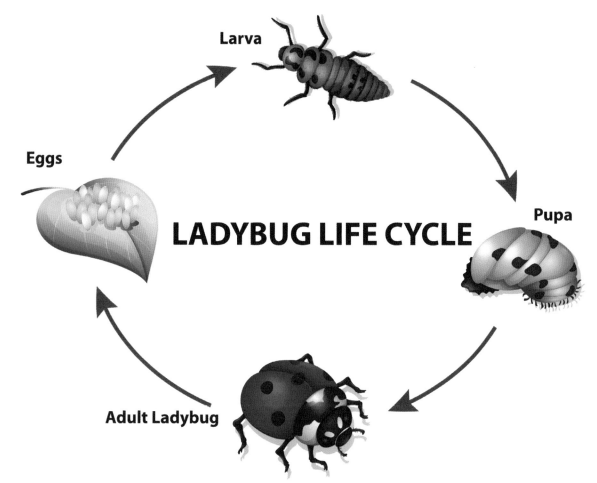

Larva

Eggs

LADYBUG LIFE CYCLE

Pupa

Adult Ladybug

5

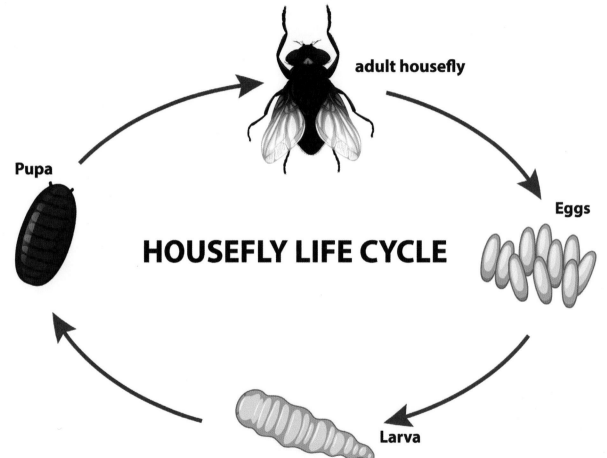

adult housefly

Pupa

HOUSEFLY LIFE CYCLE

Eggs

Larva

6

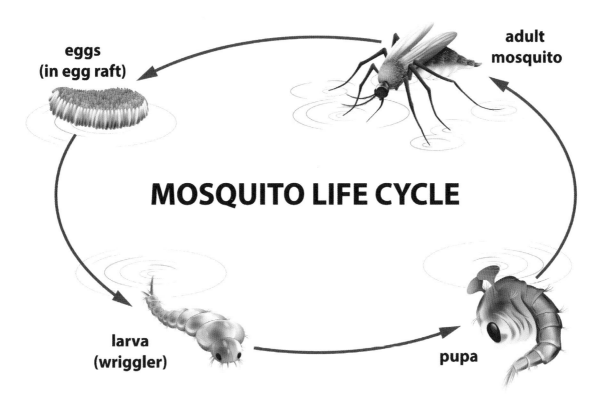

MOSQUITO LIFE CYCLE

eggs
(in egg raft)

adult
mosquito

larva
(wriggler)

pupa

7

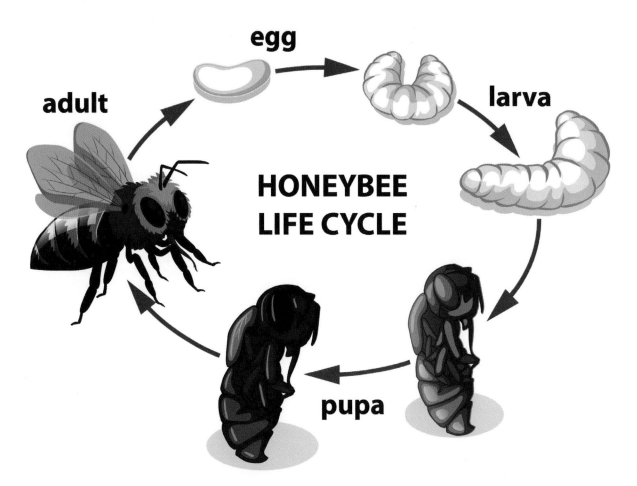

HONEYBEE LIFE CYCLE

egg

larva

pupa

adult

MEALWORM LIFE CYCLE

Eggs

Larva

Pupa

Adult

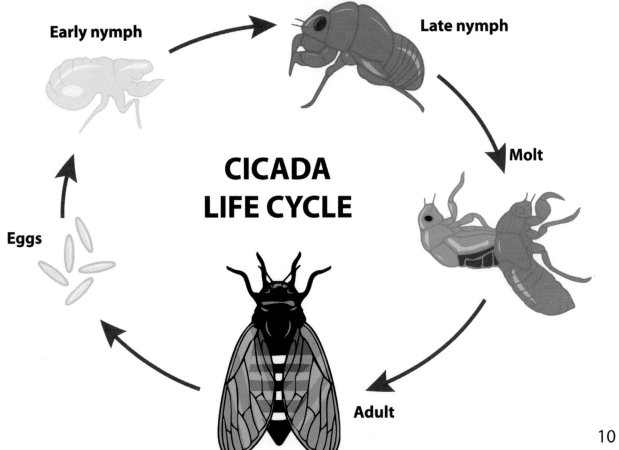

Early nymph

Late nymph

Molt

Eggs

CICADA
LIFE CYCLE

Adult

10

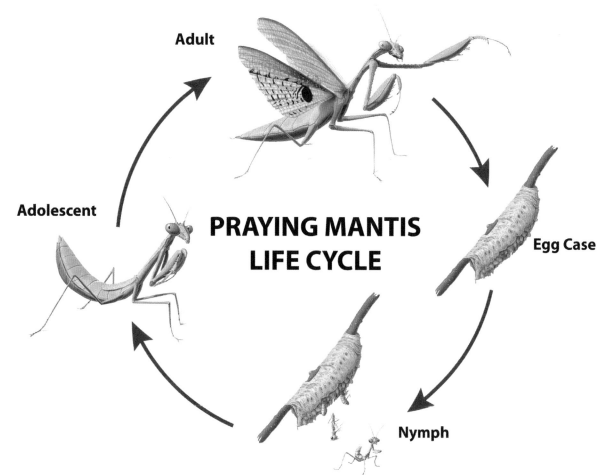

Adult

Adolescent

PRAYING MANTIS LIFE CYCLE

Egg Case

Nymph

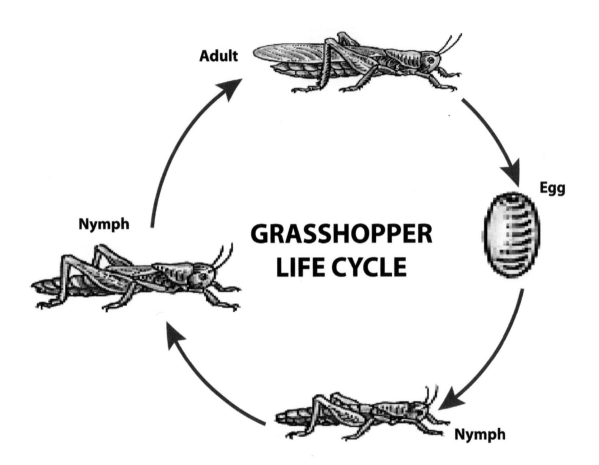

Adult

Egg

GRASSHOPPER LIFE CYCLE

Nymph

Nymph

12

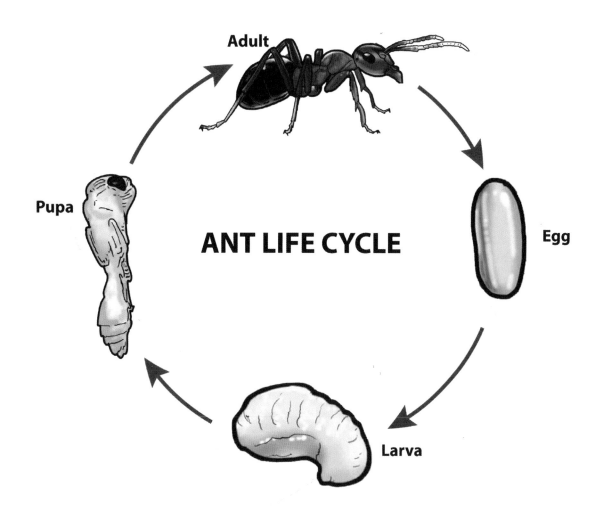

ANT LIFE CYCLE

Adult

Egg

Larva

Pupa

13

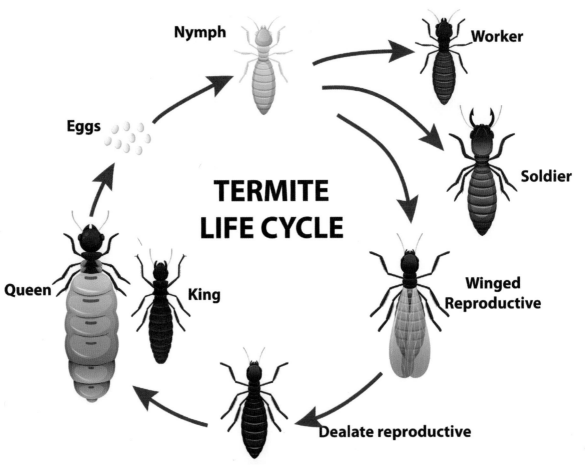

TERMITE LIFE CYCLE

Nymph

Eggs

Worker

Soldier

Winged Reproductive

Queen

King

Dealate reproductive

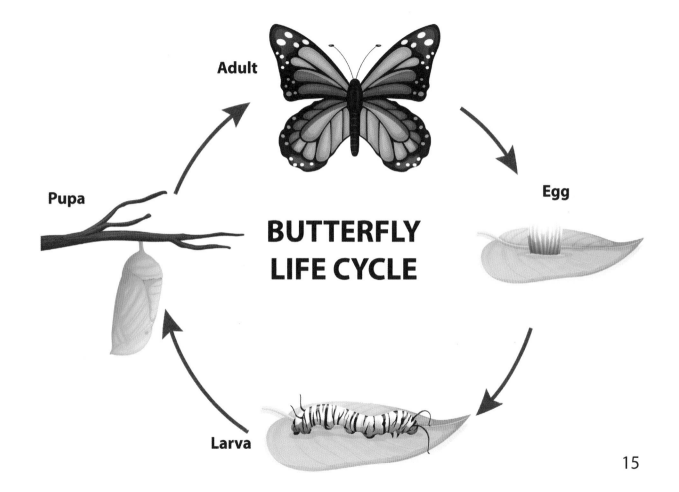

Adult

Pupa

BUTTERFLY LIFE CYCLE

Egg

Larva

15

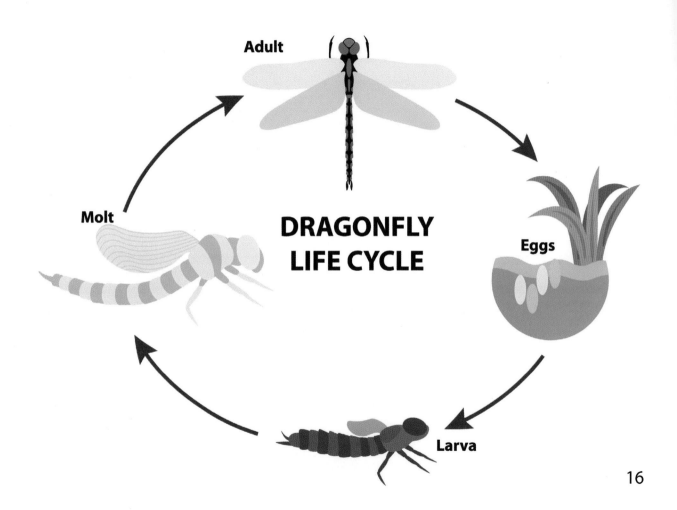

DRAGONFLY LIFE CYCLE

Adult

Eggs

Larva

Molt

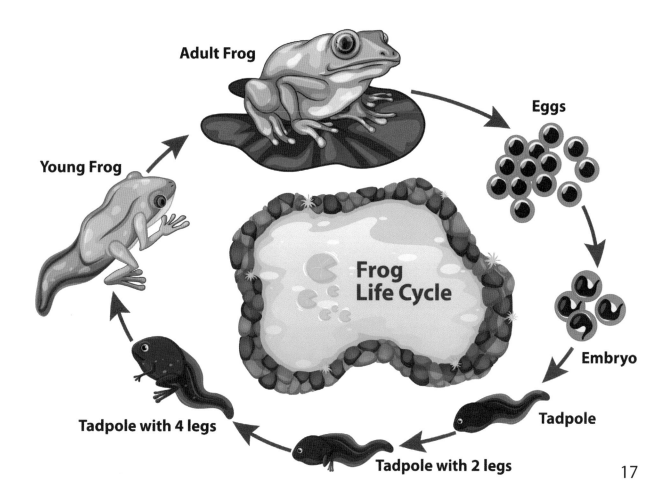

Adult Frog

Eggs

Young Frog

Frog Life Cycle

Embryo

Tadpole

Tadpole with 4 legs

Tadpole with 2 legs

17

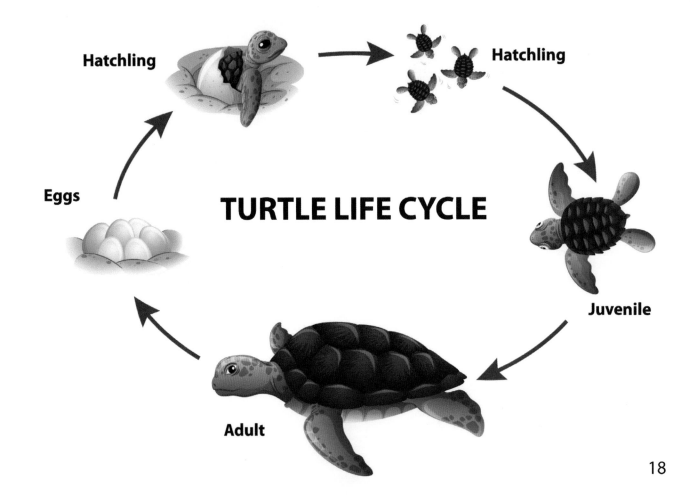

Hatchling

Hatchling

Eggs

TURTLE LIFE CYCLE

Juvenile

Adult

18

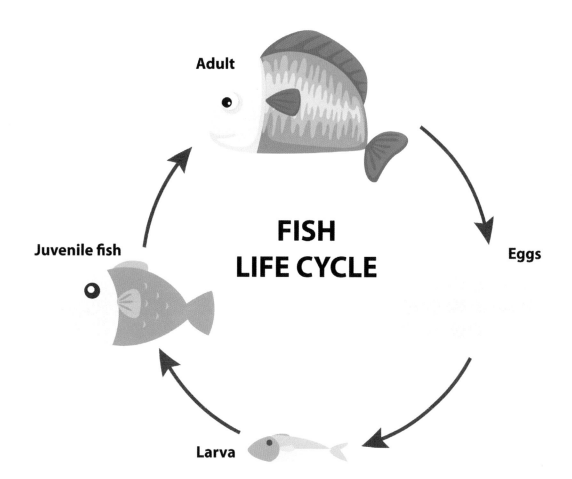

FISH LIFE CYCLE

Adult

Eggs

Larva

Juvenile fish

19

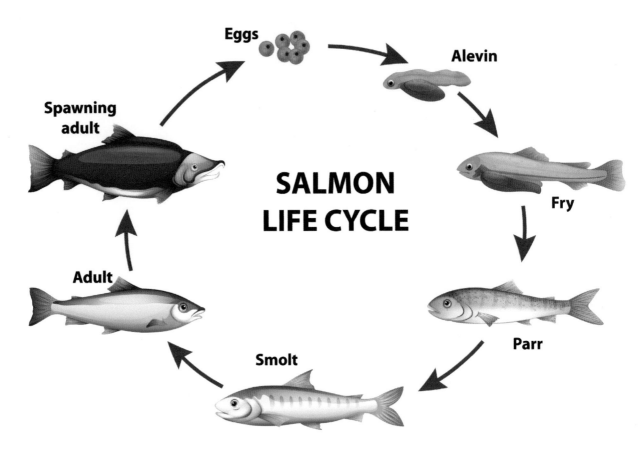

Eggs

Alevin

Spawning adult

**SALMON
LIFE CYCLE**

Fry

Adult

Parr

Smolt

20

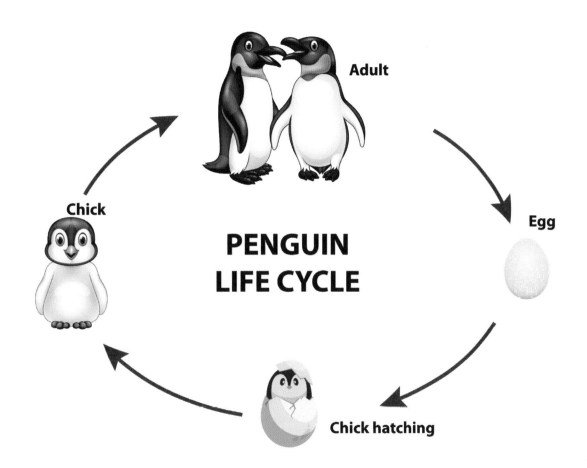

PENGUIN
LIFE CYCLE

Adult

Egg

Chick hatching

Chick

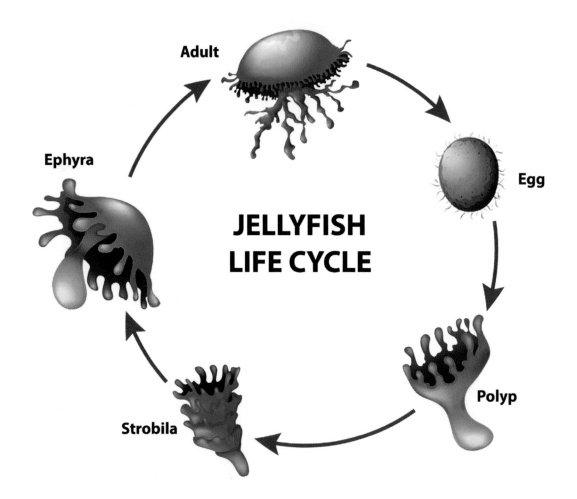

JELLYFISH LIFE CYCLE

Adult

Egg

Polyp

Strobila

Ephyra

22

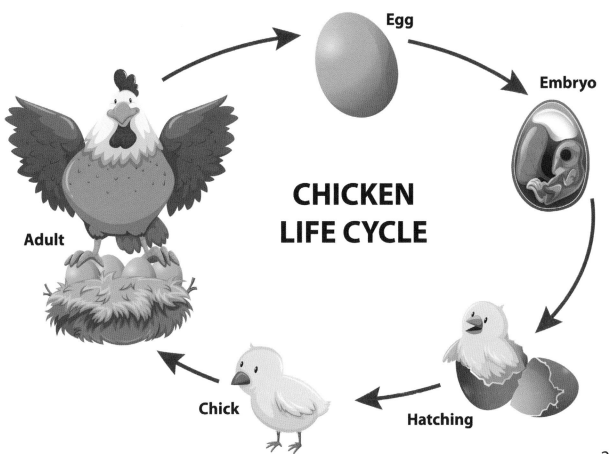

Egg

Embryo

CHICKEN
LIFE CYCLE

Adult

Chick

Hatching

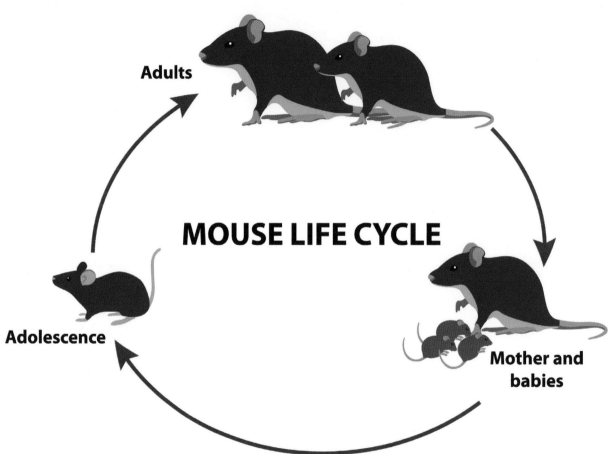

MOUSE LIFE CYCLE

Adults

Adolescence

Mother and babies

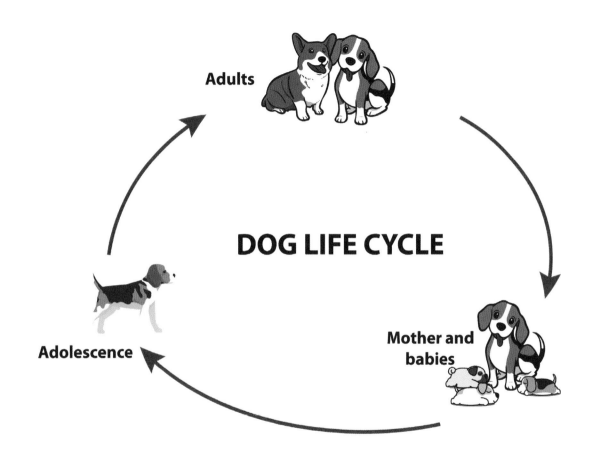

DOG LIFE CYCLE

Adults

Mother and babies

Adolescence

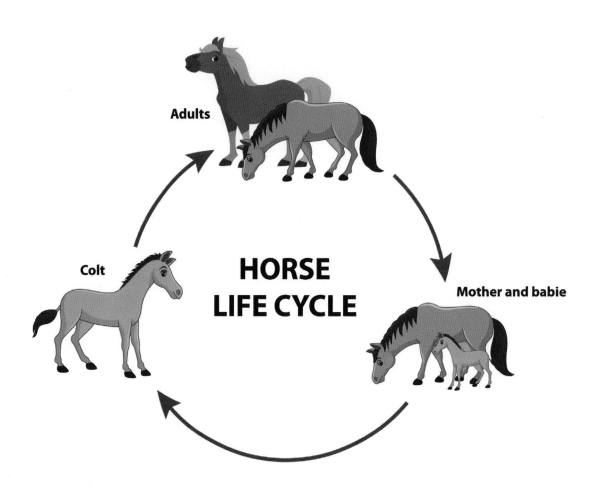

Adults

Colt

HORSE LIFE CYCLE

Mother and babie

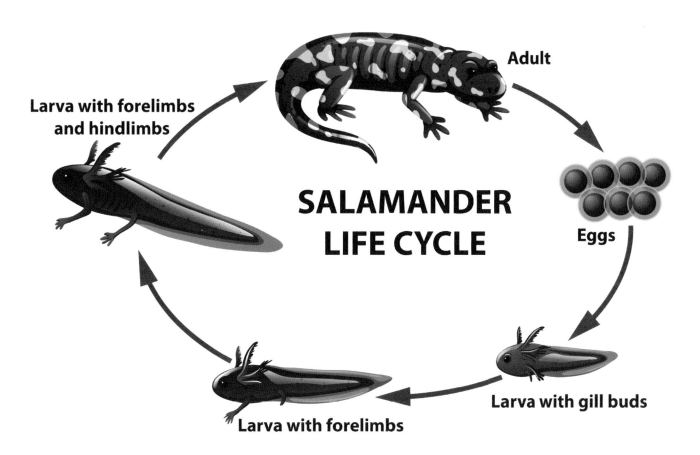

SALAMANDER LIFE CYCLE

Adult

Larva with forelimbs and hindlimbs

Eggs

Larva with gill buds

Larva with forelimbs

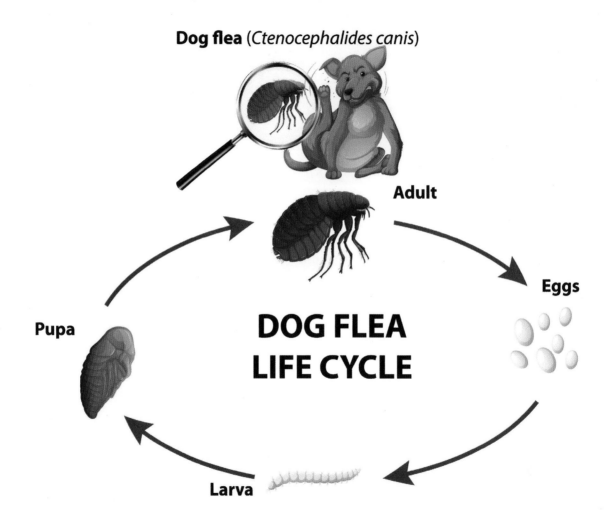

Dog flea (*Ctenocephalides canis*)

Adult

Eggs

Pupa

DOG FLEA LIFE CYCLE

Larva

28

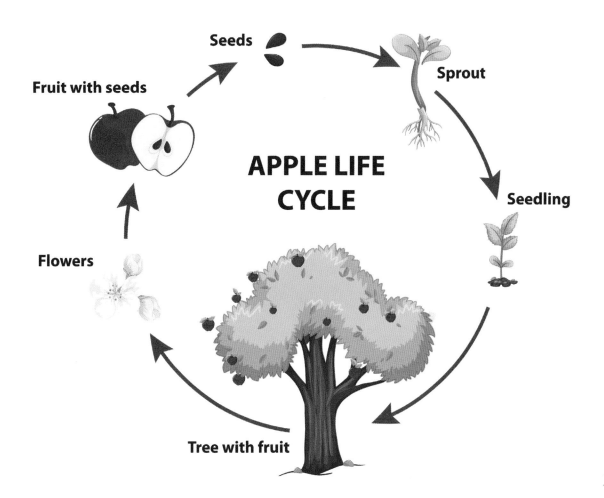

Seeds

Sprout

Fruit with seeds

APPLE LIFE CYCLE

Seedling

Flowers

Tree with fruit

29

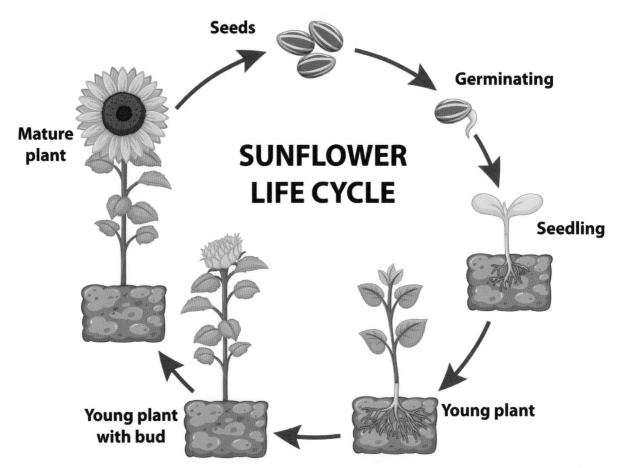

Seeds

Germinating

Mature
plant

**SUNFLOWER
LIFE CYCLE**

Seedling

Young plant

Young plant
with bud

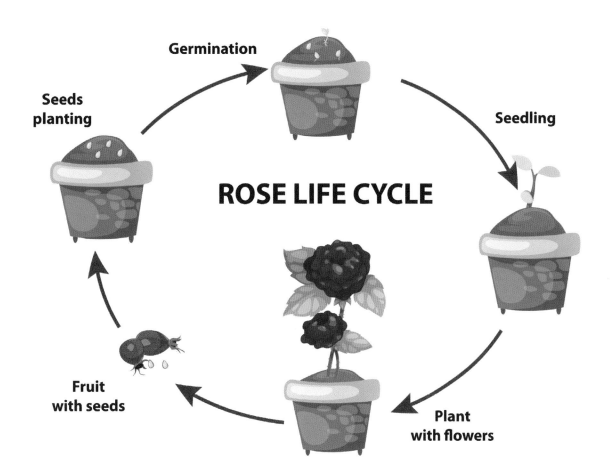

ROSE LIFE CYCLE

Seeds planting

Germination

Seedling

Plant with flowers

Fruit with seeds

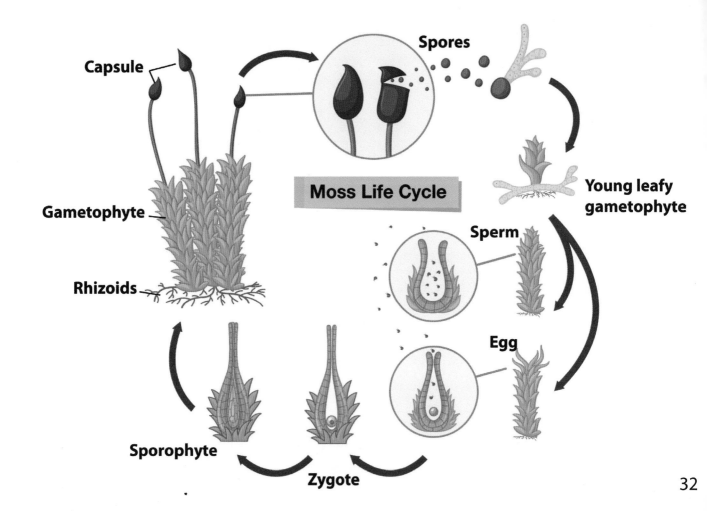

Moss Life Cycle

Capsule

Spores

Young leafy gametophyte

Gametophyte

Sperm

Rhizoids

Egg

Sporophyte

Zygote

32

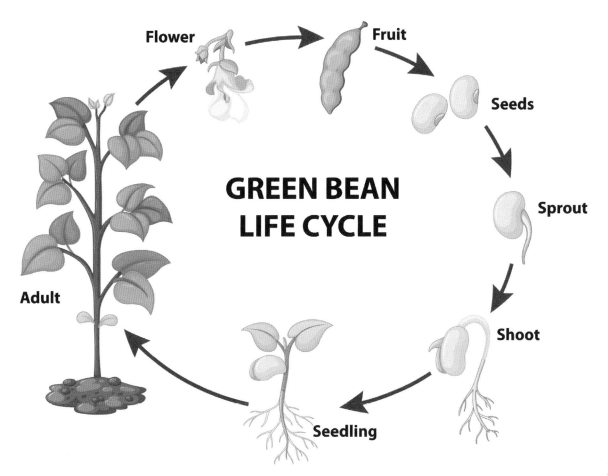

Flower

Fruit

Seeds

Sprout

Shoot

Seedling

Adult

GREEN BEAN LIFE CYCLE

33

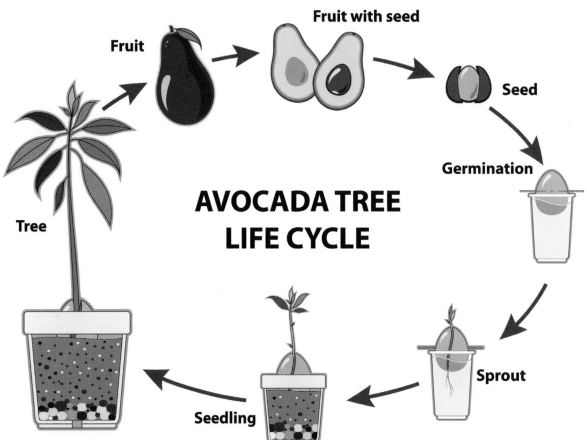

AVOCADA TREE LIFE CYCLE

Fruit

Fruit with seed

Seed

Germination

Sprout

Seedling

Tree

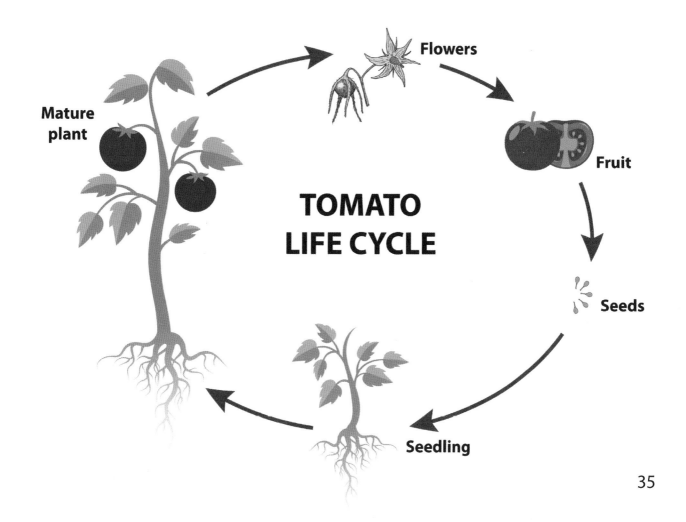

Flowers

Mature plant

TOMATO LIFE CYCLE

Fruit

Seeds

Seedling

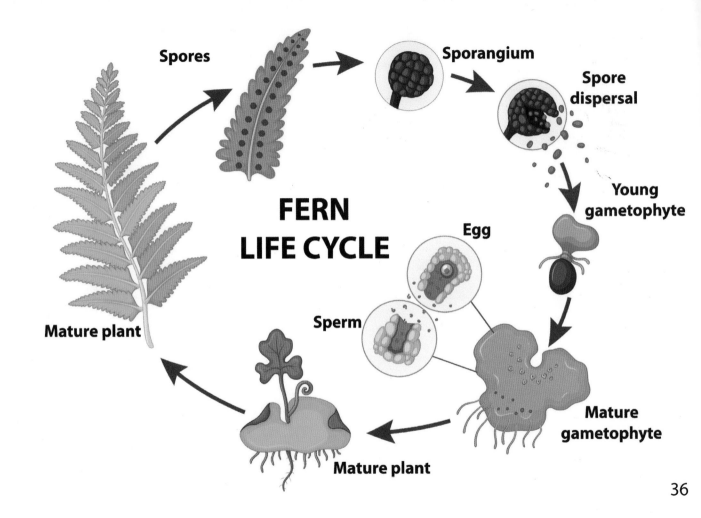

Spores

Sporangium

Spore dispersal

Young gametophyte

Egg

Sperm

FERN LIFE CYCLE

Mature plant

Mature gametophyte

Mature plant

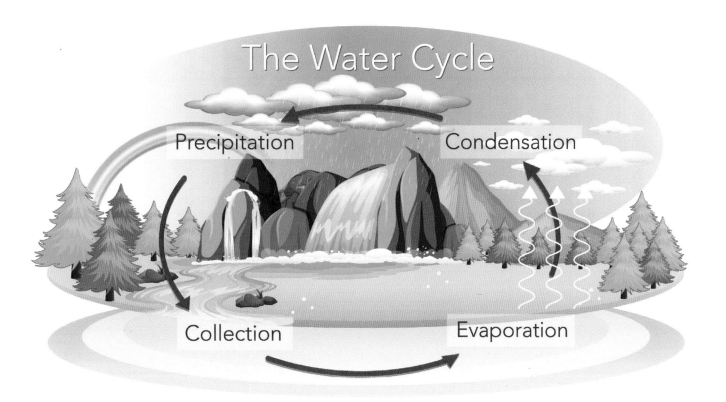

Printed in Great Britain
by Amazon